COACHING FOR ACTION

A REPORT ON LONG-TERM ADVISING IN A PROGRAM CONTEXT

COACHING FOR ACTION

A REPORT ON LONG-TERM ADVISING IN A PROGRAM CONTEXT

Victoria A. Guthrie

Center for Creative Leadership
Greensboro, North Carolina

The Center for Creative Leadership is an international, nonprofit educational institution founded in 1970 to advance the understanding, practice, and development of leadership for the benefit of society worldwide. As a part of this mission, it publishes books and reports that aim to contribute to a general process of inquiry and understanding in which ideas related to leadership are raised, exchanged, and evaluated. The ideas presented in its publications are those of the author or authors.

The Center thanks you for supporting its work through the purchase of this volume. If you have comments, suggestions, or questions about any Center publication, please contact John R. Alexander, President, at the address given below.

Center for Creative Leadership
Post Office Box 26300
Greensboro, North Carolina 27438-6300

Center for
Creative Leadership

leadership. learning. life.

CCL No. 181

Library of Congress Cataloging-in-Publication Data

Guthrie, Victoria A.
    Coaching for action : a report on long-term advising in a program context / by
    Victoria A. Guthrie.
        p. cm.
    Includes bibliographical references.
    ISBN 1-882197-50-X
    1. Executives—Training of. 2. Mentoring. I. Title.
    HD30.4.G87 1999
    658.4'07124—dc21   99-22975
                                                                        CIP

v

Table of Contents

Preface

The purpose of this report is to document some important lessons that we at the Center for Creative Leadership (CCL) have learned about enhancing development in the work setting. Our findings enable CCL to add elements to leadership development program delivery that reinforce the participants' learnings from the classroom experience. One of the elements included in several CCL programs is the coaching-and-support role of *process advisor* (PA). The process advisor works closely with the participant to help him or her understand and develop his or her goals, both during the program and for a period of time following it; and the advisor-advisee partnership will span anywhere from six months to a year.

The PA concept has been part of the Awareness Program for Executive Excellence (APEX)®, the custom program for Florida School Superintendents, programs for specific clients in various industries, and LeaderLab®. Because it has been an especially strong element in LeaderLab, where we have been able to follow the development of the concept for ten years, this report will focus on our learnings about the PA process within this program. LeaderLab is an action-learning program based on client surveys of the training needs and challenges of organizations and on state-of-the-art research in the field. The role of the PA in this program is to continue the assessment begun in the survey, determine the level of challenge, and support the participant during his or her developmental process. Because the program spans a period of six months, the PA element fits into it particularly well.

Over the years that the PA role has been used in LeaderLab, CCL has studied its origins, observed its impact, and considered the ways that it can be used in other settings. Throughout that time, I discovered that human resource (HR) people, program designers, organizations who use leadership development programs, and others wished to know more about the PA role. This publication provides a historical description of the Center's experiences with the process advisor model.

I would like to acknowledge many people who supported and guided me through this work. First, of course, the process advisors themselves and especially Joyce Richman, Beth Dixson, and Connie Grant. Thanks also go to the reviewers who read early versions of this manuscript, Harvette Dixon, Robert E. Kaplan, Mary A. Michaud, and Roland Nelson. Colleagues who advised me early on in the writing process include Cindy McCauley, Bill Morley, Michael Wakefield, Raoul Buron, Cheryl DeCiantis, and Sue Kennedy. Thanks also to them. And finally, I'd like to thank my husband, Kevin, whose steadfast support makes all endeavors possible.

Introduction

An important part of any development experience for managers is to have other people help them clearly define their goals and support their efforts toward achieving them. There are a variety of ways to do this—coaching, mentoring, giving on-the-spot feedback, encouraging, and so forth. This report describes a type of advocate role, called *process advisor* (PA), that was developed specifically for individuals undergoing developmental experiences in CCL's LeaderLab program (the PA concept has subsequently been used in other settings). Because of its underlying design and its six-month-long format, LeaderLab needed a support role that was more comprehensive than the traditional ones of feedback-giving, reinforcing, acting as a role model, and so forth.

The process advisor concept, as designed for LeaderLab, aims to help the advisee (1) learn with and from the PA, (2) tap into effective learning as it occurs, and (3) be more attuned to situations in order to deal with ambiguity and take effective action. It does so by providing the opportunity for individuals to benefit from the expertise of another, develop their leadership skills, move from traditional management-by-objective thinking to process management thinking, and revisit and expand their mental models of how the world and people operate.

This report describes CCL's experience with process advising, primarily through its use in the LeaderLab program. The first segment of the report documents the thinking that went into the program design by describing how and why CCL developed the PA role and outlining the philosophy that underpins the role of the PA in assisting the participant to carry out more effective actions in work situations and sustain the developmental process over time.

The remainder of the report documents some of the key issues and learnings CCL has accumulated since it began using the PA concept in l990. I examine what PAs do and the roles they play, how to be a more effective PA, PA learnings to date, and other uses and mediums to be used with the process advising and coaching methodologies. The last section offers a brief developmental relationship assessment exercise, focusing on the types and intent of various coaching roles.

In a series of appendices following the main body of this report, I include descriptive materials about CCL's LeaderLab program and some of its tools. I also collect statements from participants that shed light on the process advisor experience from a different perspective and present a case study of one participant's progress during the long-term advising relationship. This material is provided to give a deeper and more rounded view of the process advisor role and the benefit it can bring to development programs.

Although this is not a how-to report, practitioners who have administered coaching programs or have been the subjects of them will find its information helpful when planning new initiatives around support for development.

Why Process Advisors Are Important to Development

CCL has spent the last twenty-five years creating a learning environment that facilitates effective leadership development. It comprises these three elements: assessment, challenge, and support (McCauley, Moxley, & Van Velsor, 1998). When combined, these elements make a developmental experience more powerful.

The Center's View of Development

Assessment provides a means for participants to take a deep look at their individual capabilities, their strengths and developmental needs, and their interactions with others.

Challenge means surfacing participants' mental models and paradigms about leadership effectiveness and encouraging them to explore different ways of thinking. Participants are challenged with experiences that demand skills and abilities beyond their current capabilities, with situations that are confusing or ambiguous, and with situations they would rather not deal with.

Support is a key factor in maintaining motivation to learn and grow. It helps engender a belief that one can learn, grow, and change. Support also helps people handle the struggle and pain of developing, that is, bear the weight of the experience. It helps them maintain a positive view of themselves as people capable of dealing with challenges. Seeing that others place a positive value on their efforts to change and grow is a key factor in people's decisions to stay on course with developmental goals.

Leadership development is a process that requires both a variety of developmental experiences (which involve assessment, active challenge, and support) and the ability to learn (which is the element that the individual brings to the development process). These two factors, the variety of developmental experiences and the ability to learn, have a direct impact on each other. A third factor also has an impact: the organizational context, that is, the organization's business strategy, systems, culture, and so forth.

Thus, in CCL's understanding of human development, leadership development creates a variety of rich, developmental experiences that each provide assessment, challenge, and support; enhances people's ability to learn from experience in a more immediate and useful manner; and uses approaches that integrate the learnings and various developmental experiences and embeds them in the organizational context.

Given this approach, CCL knew it was important to develop a method that allowed participants to deal with the dynamic tension between the demands of various work situations and an ability to clearly articulate a sense of purpose from three perspectives: as an individual, as a leader of a team or group, and as a contributing member of an organization. CCL also knew that a high-quality leadership development system would support action learning and be flexible enough to respond to rapid change.

To address the need for flexibility, we designed an action learning program, LeaderLab (see the program description in Appendix A), that moved beyond a one-time training event to a multisession interaction. This program design included methods and tools to enhance an individual's ability to learn from experience in the work setting over time as he or she interacted with employees and worked through challenges. The processes we developed aimed to help people change or adapt behaviors or attitudes that would be more effective for both the individual and the organization. The PA was one of those processes.

The intended goal for both the program and the process advising work was to encourage and enable the individual to take more effective actions in his or her leadership situations—actions that develop the individual and others in the pursuit of goals that benefit all.

What the Clients Wanted from Development Training

As CCL began its design work on LeaderLab, it was clear about what it believed it needed to do as far as creating support roles for development, but what did the Center's clients expect? To find out, a two-part survey (Burnside & Guthrie, 1992) asked, first, what organizations needed from training and development as they moved into the next century.

Appendix G summarizes results of this part of the survey. What the clients needed and wanted can be summed up by one respondent's succinct response: "We want development experiences that go beyond awareness and move to action; that go beyond teaching heads to moving feet."

The second part of the client survey asked respondents to describe the challenges organizations were facing as they looked to the twenty-first century. Responses were organized into four categories: change, diverse people and thinking, building the future, and turbulence.

Change. Clients responded that the challenge of change is that it is rapid, substantive, and ongoing.

Diverse People and Thinking. Clients said that demographics are shifting. Mergers, acquisitions, and reorganizations place various professional groups with different perspectives on work teams and projects that are critical to organizational success.

Building the Future. The respondents' comments centered around the task of building a shared sense of purpose for the future work of the organization.

Turbulence. Further studies (Young & Dixon, 1996) enabled CCL to clearly articulate the types of events in an individual's situation that make up a large part of this challenge. Defined as unanticipated occurrences that command the attention of the participant and are typically stressful (Gryskiewicz, 1999), turbulence was manifested in four areas:

1. *System.* These events included such things as downsizing, reorganization, and the replacement of senior management. Participants appeared to have little impact on these occurrences although they were greatly affected by them.

2. *Job specific.* Major events in this area were taking a new job within the same organization, sometimes as a result of a system-level change; taking a job in a new organization; and job loss, again often due to a systemic change such as moving between line and staff positions.

3. *Personal.* These were events that generally happened outside the workplace yet greatly affected how a participant functioned at work. Included among them were personal health problems or those of family members, the loss of a close relationship through separation or death, and the instigation of new relationships or resumption of a former one.

4. *Psychological.* These events involved long-standing problems, such as alcoholism, depression, and chemical imbalance, and the effort of the individual to learn to deal with the issue in a new way or to gain new insight into the impact of the problem on his or her work.

Meeting the Challenge of Development

CCL now understood that it needed to design a process in which participants could experience the chaos and rapid changes affecting their work environment while using their own situations and challenges as the basis for understanding and action. In taking the next step, the Center combined what it knew from its experience and research, what clients were saying, and learnings gained from the work of Dr. Leonard Sayles (1993) and others.

That step was to create a foundation of seven competencies to which all involved in the program could adhere. In building this foundation, CCL determined that there were two master competencies that acted as brackets to hold and guide the five other competencies.

The two master competencies were (1) the ability to clarify and maintain a sense of purpose for various aspects of each participant's life and (2) the ability to learn how to learn.

In this context purpose can be seen as the area of interaction that lies between an individual's thoughts, feelings, and actions and the way he or she chooses to interact with the various situations in life and work—as an individual, a team or group leader, and a contributing member of an organization. Purpose is not static but dynamic, as the individual must constantly deal with various situations.

In defining this competency, CCL also envisioned a program role that would assist participants in clarifying a sense of purpose and understanding how to deal with experiences while becoming more conscious of the choices and actions that need to be made.

Learning to learn requires us to take something of value from our experiences. Learning isn't automatic. All of us tend to be prisoners of our successful habits. Successful learning requires going against the grain, pushing beyond the comfort zone.

How an individual approaches a situation and his or her ability to learn from experience are the best predictors of management success. When a person tackles a problem differently from the way he or she has dealt with the problem before, that person increases his or her ability to handle other problems.

Good learners don't simply learn behaviors; they learn new *actions*. That kind of learning is hard. So CCL saw the need for a program role that would provide the support and advocacy necessary to achieve this new learning by assisting the participants with tough, varied challenges that encourage overcoming previously successful habits with a learned new behavior.

Balanced between these two core abilities, the five other competencies CCL created include the ability to (1) deal effectively with interpersonal relationships, (2) think and behave in terms of systems, (3) approach decision-making from the standpoint of trade-offs, (4) think and act with flexibility, and (5) maintain emotional balance by coping with disequilibrium. Table 1 provides details on each of these five competencies.

Creating the Process Advisor

Now that CCL had created a baseline understanding of the seven competencies necessary for the development process, it proceeded to consider a name and a definition for the role that was necessary to play within the LeaderLab program as participants were guided and helped through their program endeavors.

Naming and Defining the Process Advisor

Given what we knew about developmental action learning, we felt that the word *process*—defined as a natural phenomenon marked by gradual changes that lead toward a particular result—was at the core of programs like LeaderLab that emphasize development or training programs for future action. We wanted the role to be a blend of advocate, partisan, and adherent. And the best word to combine the support, assistance, fidelity, loyalty, and help in keeping the process we envisioned going would be *advisor*.

We also knew it would be important for the advisors to help individuals move from an event-focused perspective to understanding and operating from a process perspective, that is, to help them develop a deeper understanding of the interconnectedness of the various aspects of leading and organizational systems and their own impact and effect in their leadership situations. The name we gave to our particular view of this advocate captured both of these goals—*process advisor*.

One issue that arose during this naming process was CCL's desire to maintain the distinction between process advisor and coach. Clients' actual needs in training indicated that the tasks in the PA role would call for the talents of the coach, counsel, consultant, mentor, and feedback provider in various combinations. So it became necessary to sort out the various reactions to the term *process advisor* for those who were used to using the above terms (especially coach) to define people in development support roles.

Table 1
Five Leadership Competencies in the Process Advisor Experience

Competency	*Components for Mastery*
Deal effectively with interpersonal relationships.	Manage the face-to-face interactions; manage systemwide interactions; and deal with people very different from oneself and effectively handle those differences.
Think and behave in terms of systems.	Recognize that an organization is an organic whole and even "minor" change in one part of it affects it as a whole.
Approach decision-making from the standpoint of trade-offs.	Understand that even though traditional maximization approaches can be useful in understanding the complexity of decision-making, decisions always involve multiple competing points of view and conflict; to focus each decision on what the situation calls for, be able to accurately weigh the ethical dilemmas faced when leading.
Think and act with flexibility.	Moderate and adapt one's thinking and action quickly and effectively as new information or situations arise.
Maintain emotional balance by coping with disequilibrium.	Recognize the leader's need for emotional competency; develop the ability to see conditions realistically; learn to be aware of one's own emotions and the feelings of others and to actively build support in one's situation.

For some the PA label is more palatable than coach, but for others, coach is a generic term that blankets any type of relational process within the context of development work. This became very clear at one organization when the president immediately dismissed the idea of coaching, stating that when he heard the word coach he thought of teaching someone something— like a sport or how to sell. He saw coach as meaning overseer or someone charged with telling others what to do successfully. However when the concept of the PA was explained, he felt that was exactly what the organization needed.

When CCL considered the definition of the PA role in LeaderLab, the image that consistently emerged in discussion was of someone who is a key advocate (see Table 2) for an individual in a real-time developmental relationship during a multisession, ongoing program that officially spans a specified amount of time (in this case, approximately six to nine months). This is the premise we have used throughout our experience with the program.

Table 2
Process Advisor as Advocate

Advisee	*Process Advisor*
Decides on action plans and development needs.	Helps clarify strengths and potential blocks.
Evaluates progress and learning.	Provides perspective and gives feedback.
Owns the situation and finds own solutions.	Inquires, probes, supports; does not provide answers.

The Tasks of the Process Advisor

The goal of the six-month LeaderLab program is to encourage and enable individuals to take more effective actions; the PA's major job within that context is to continually focus participants on asking themselves important questions, the two primary ones being: (1) What does the situation call for from me as an individual, as a team/group leader, as a contributing member of an organization? (2) What is the ideal or purpose I am striving for?

These two questions lead to what we call *anchors*, the baseline principles of the PA's job that guide his or her activities. Table 3 details the anchors that moor the process advisor in a long-term developmental relationship with a client.

Table 3
Anchors for Process Advisors

Six-month process goal	Encourage and enable individual to take more effective actions in leadership situations, actions that develop individuals and others in pursuit of goals that benefit all.
Sense of purpose	Help individual clarify the vision for his or her specific leadership situation through review of his or her life biography. Help individual deal with the questions: What is the ideal I am striving for—as an individual, as a leader of a team or group, as a contributing member of an organization? What does my leadership situation call for from me?
Learning from experience	Help individual become a more effective learner by encouraging him or her to identify blocks to learning, and supporting efforts to overcome them.
Leadership competencies	Help individual practice five leadership competencies: have effective personal relations with people different from oneself, adopt a systems approach to his or her situation, deal with decision-making in terms of trade-offs, cope with emotional disequilibrium, and maintain flexibility in thoughts and actions.

The PA role is designed to help participants address problems that arise in the implementation of action plans and to provide encouragement with these plans. PAs are advocates for the work the participant is doing, offering fidelity, loyalty, and a steady and firm backing for that work. The PA role is a blend of expert, confidante, cop, cheerleader, champion, and counselor. PAs listen, recommend, encourage, inform, suggest, counsel, challenge, and support. Their roles will be described in more detail later in this report.

The Tools of the Process Advisor

PAs guide each participant's development within the frame of the program. In this particular design, the program's overarching goal is to encourage and enable the individual to take more effective actions in his or her leadership situations, actions that develop the individual and others in pursuit of goals that benefit all.

To help participants achieve this, PAs use the competencies-and-challenges framework, the program itself, and a prework package of data that participants complete prior to the program. Figure 1 shows how and when the PA comes into the long-term leadership developmental relationship.

The prework packet consists of a number of qualitative and quantitative surveys. Qualitative feedback instruments, such as situation audits, help individuals describe a sense of purpose from individual, group, and organizational perspectives; help clarify perceptions of various groups toward one another; establish operating norms for the group; and articulate the top ten issues facing the participant and identify whether each issue is an individual, group/team, or organizational one. Life biography and life-transition work are the focus of additional qualitative surveys. Advisees often reported back additional insight from these surveys that suggests a heightened self-awareness.

The quantitative feedback consists of a number of self-assessment surveys, such as FIRO-B, the Success Style Profile, and the Jones Inventory of Barriers; and 360-degree instruments, such as Benchmarks® and KEYS®. PAs prepare diligently by poring over notes and feedback materials, and participants often report a satisfaction with that preparation. As one participant put it: "[The PA] gave me a breathing image of the data from a static interpretation of the data. She had done her homework and asked excellent questions."

Although working with the hard data is one portion of the first face-to-face meeting, PAs generally report that after the first session the individual moves to real-life situations and an analysis of actions that can be done and that need to be done. The instruments are used later only to challenge or confirm a participant's self-understanding.

The learning journal is another tool the PA reviews and uses over the developmental process and relationship to better understand and connect conversations, actions, and discussions. We use the term *journal* rather loosely to mean any recording method that helps the individual keep a running account of daily thoughts and reflections. The journal allows the PA and the participant to examine the strategies, successes, pitfalls, and stress points that often accompany the learning process. Specifically, a journal provides three benefits: It is (1) a mechanism for reflection—a means for the participant to build the skill of learning from experience, (2) a means of building data that enable the PA to be more helpful and allow the participant the opportunity over time to look for patterns and trends in his or her leadership, and (3) a means to better self-understanding by bringing insight through

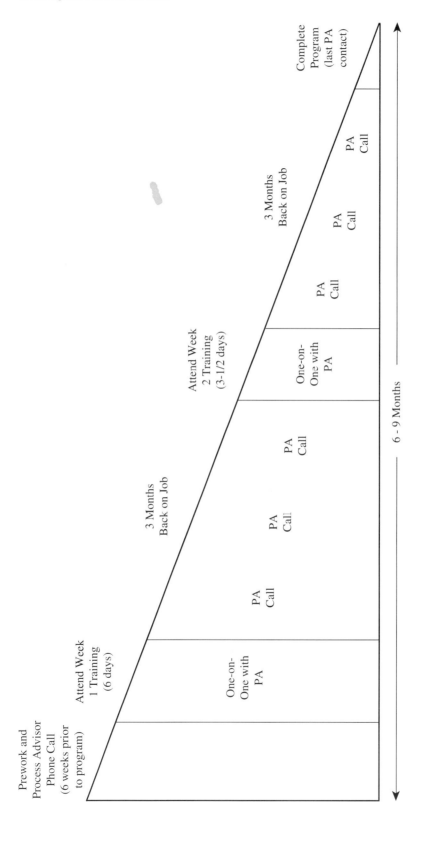

Figure 1
LeaderLab/PA Design Flow

reflection. (Appendix B provides more detail on why the learning journal is part of the PA process.)

Participants are provided with journals for use during their on-site meetings and during the months between sessions. The intent of the journals is to help participants develop a systematic reflection process, to establish a routine whereby they capture not only what but *how* they learned and, further, periodically review and reflect on those reflections. Participants are encouraged to find their own time, place, and format for the learning journal. They are free to use a computer, a tape recorder, a paper outline, or any other method that is comfortable and familiar.

Although the benefits are well proven and the means of keeping a journal are completely open, some advisees don't like or want to use the journal. A typical comment from one group: "It seems to have taken most of us the first two to three months to learn how to effectively write and use our journals."

Other participants report that the journal seems to be integral to this type of coaching. In one advisee's words: "Through this process, I have been enormously encouraged and enabled in my work over these past six months. The most helpful thing is talking with the PA about my entries because the writing and the discussing of those writings helped me to reflect on events and work things out in a reflective mode. However, it was the PA that brought the insight that I needed to think about the situation more fully, less defensively and to keep my sense of perspective. It's easy to become self-critical and despondent when reflecting rather than to celebrate the differences and the PA helped keep my ego intact in the process."

The following excerpts from one participant's summary of her journal keeping experience also illustrate some of the benefits (the entire essay is reproduced in Appendix C).

> The journal has served two distinct purposes for me. Because of the reflective nature of journaling, I am less critical of myself and others. I have also learned to extract "pearls of wisdom" from the learnings. I discovered a different way to approach the problem or was able to "cut my losses" without feeling a sense of loss. My process advisor and I concur that I have grown and changed in a very positive and noticeable manner over these six months—and my change partners agree. . . .

> The insights I garnered over the first three months were obvious in others as I returned for the second session. Listening to my peers and

watching their developmental level was a reaffirmation of my personal growth. I was cognizant of a gain in confidence, listening skills, and open and honest feedback. . . .

My final and most important "aha" resulted from the journal. I learned that the process of sharing my thoughts, feelings and philosophies worked for me. The PA's reception of these musings has affirmed my ability to write for publication. I do plan to submit a compilation of these entries as a published manuscript. I will use this gift from God— the ability to paint pictures with a pen—to spread my message.

The Roles of the Process Advisor

The specific roles of the PAs were not immediately evident to CCL during the time it was conceptualizing the role of PA. But as CCL gained experience with using PAs, a number of specific roles did emerge to replace earlier generalizations.

The PA roles can be grouped using the assessment, challenge, and support model of leadership development. Within each of these modules, the PA's role covers different facets of the developmental relationship (McCauley et al., 1998, pp. 160-193):

- Assessment: feedback provider, reflective thinking partner, expert
- Challenge: dialogue partner, accountant
- Support: role model, counselor, positive reinforcer, historian

How the PA performs within these relationships and the connection between process advising and leadership development are described below.

Expert. The PA's expertise is almost always in process development and adult learning, and is most appropriate when managers attempt to make personal changes that may be difficult for them. This is because these changes involve altering ingrained behavioral patterns, long-held beliefs or traits that are reinforced in the work or home setting. The PA's expertise is different although not mutually exclusive from *content expertise*, which is generally subject related. It is appropriate for managers who are inexperienced in a role or whose job success potential would benefit from the perspective of someone who has been in a similar position.

The PA's expertise is anchored to the goal and competencies being focused on in the LeaderLab developmental experience, and PAs are knowledgeable about the participant through the prework assessments. Also, PAs have an understanding of the advisee's situation and the action plan he or she is working on. A PA asks questions, suggests ideas and alternate strategies,

provides insight, and helps identify patterns of behavior, especially through
the journal writing exercise.

Reflective Thinking Partner. PAs engage the individual in reflective
thinking by probing assumptions, hypothesizing about outcomes, challenging,
serving as a sounding board, and providing different perspectives. The use of
a journal is one tool they use over time to help in this process to capture
thinking, explore ideas and feelings, and become aware of patterns. From a
PA perspective, the advisees who use the journal gain a great deal from
LeaderLab. Patterns become more evident, and they see progress more
clearly. Writing in the journal allows depth in both the discovery process for
the individual and the ongoing information for the PA as they conduct the
telephone conference calls that are part of the program.

The reflective thinking partner can be especially helpful to individuals—especially those working in global environments—as they review their
mental models and understanding of the world. For example, Sebastian (all
names in this report are pseudonyms) was a very capable and bright high-
potential in his international organization. At the start of the six-month
process, he would often pull back from a discussion group or even get up and
walk away. After all, what did these others know of his world?

The first three months with his PA were rocky: He would reschedule
phone appointments, saw no value in the use of a journal, and held fast to
what others needed to be doing to make his work effective. It was not until
the second face-to-face meeting with his PA that he began to understand that
all the change he hoped to effect in the organization had to begin with him—
how he saw the world, how he interacted with others, and so forth. At the end
of that meeting, he commented how he finally "got it. My PA had been trying
to help me slow down and reflect and reframe my issues." He intended to use
their next three months together far more effectively.

Feedback Provider. In addition to providing expertise around the
assessments used in the program, the PA provides honest feedback about the
individual's actions. Through interactions with the advisee and through
observations during the two program sessions, the PA is able to cite examples
and raise awareness in a very tangible, focused manner. Through giving
feedback, the PA helps the individual wrestle with resolving skill deficiencies
or developing strengths that the individual was not fully utilizing.

As the relationship moves from the program setting to the workplace,
the PA also takes the role of *feedback interpreter*. Here the PA helps the
individual work through on-the-job challenges and helps him or her address

interpersonal issues and blocks in learning. The PA then helps the individual strategize ways to remove blocks or confront them.

Dialogue Partner. "I do feel encouraged and enabled to work towards the expanded vision. I have really been struggling with how to develop a shared vision and have been very blocked by this. I finally had a breakthrough this morning when I talked with my PA and we reframed my vision as a quest, a treasure hunt with my group to develop a shared sense of purpose. Once I was able to make my vision an activity rather than a thing, I felt I could finally move on with it. The work with the PA enabled me to ask the questions and identify the actions I need to take. I am most hopeful about starting this process (especially knowing I have a sounding board in my PA), even with my current group (which will change in the next couple of months). I am looking forward to helping spread this throughout the organization (planting seeds). My PA and I spent time discussing how I can maintain the energy to sustain this in the face of the radical changes we are undergoing." With the PA in the role of dialogue partner, the participant takes responsibility for drawing conclusions and deciding upon a course of action.

Participant ownership of issues and decisions can be a difficult and a real going-against-the-grain experience. Frequently, participants expect their PA to have the answers, to tell them what to do, especially if they are struggling through a particularly difficult work time. As in the expert and reflective thinking roles, in the dialogue partner role the PA places the burden of learning and change on the participant.

The PA also frequently serves as a *practice partner*, enabling the individual to role-play interactions or scenarios from a number of different angles.

Accountant. In this role, the PA holds the participant responsible for actions and program action plans. The PA uses the original plan as a framework; however, he or she also recognizes the evolutionary nature of the corporate world today and does not drive the action plan as it was originally written.

For many participants, that surprise flexibility turns to awareness of how their work groups respond to today's fast pace; then they begin thinking of ways to help their teams recognize and celebrate progress.

Positive Reinforcer. "The PA helped me visualize needed changes and showed me how to focus on where and how in accomplishing my goals."

The PA provides affirmation, praise, and encouragement when participants attempt to make changes. The PA expresses confidence in the individual, and through support, honest feedback, and expertise or knowledge about the process, he or she models the behavior asked of the individual in an exercise, involving three people in the class and three people in their work environment.

This support role and the next (counselor) reflect the increasing sense of turbulence and stress individuals bring to the interactions. In the past, the question was, How do I get to the next level? Now, with the conditions of employment changing and the pace of work ever increasing, the questions tend to be, What do I do well? What needs to change, develop, or grow?

Counselor. In this role, the PA helps the individual confront and deal with the emotional side of change and development, especially when that person is experiencing major shifts in role and/or responsibility in his organization. The PA provides support, not as an advice-giver but as a listener who can help the individual develop appropriate strategies to deal with the rapid and substantive change. These dialogues enable the individual, with the PA's help, to tap into his or her own authenticity. Feelings are evaluated, and the PA is used as a safe person with whom the participant can vent frustration and anger and examine issues of balancing work, family, and community responsibilities.

As one participant said, "The PA had no vested interest, so there was an impartial point of view. He helped me be clear on what I was thinking around issues at work."

Historian. Although not employed as often as the other PA roles, the role of historian makes an important contribution to the individual's developmental learning. At times participants are going so fast in their day-to-day working life, they are surprised when PAs remind them what they were thinking and doing two and three months before and how far they've come.

Role Model. By virtue of the PA's ongoing modeling of listening skills, openness, and willingness to engage in the learning process, the advisee learns ways to do that for others in his or her organization. The interaction and modeling done by the PA throughout the relationship is helpful in the advisee's attempt to interact more effectively.

For example, one PA reported that a month before the final phone call and closure session, she asked for ideas from the participant on how to put together a positive closure session. The participant was surprised and said: "I never thought about that. I should say goodbye to a close associate next week. I usually ignore things like that even though I know it's an ending. This will give me a model for how to get better closure with people."

All of these roles have been used alone or in combination in LeaderLab. For examples, see Appendix D. Although the participants do not discuss PA tasks as "roles," Appendix E offers a collection of the most frequently stated advisee viewpoints following their six-month experiences. Their comments nevertheless capture the variety of roles played by the PA.

Beyond these roles, contact with the PA following LeaderLab is seen as one of the most important parts of the program. The advisee sees the PA as the one constant in the ever-changing work environment, the person who provides continuity throughout the entire development process.

It may be that the PA's perceived objectivity and acceptance and positive regard for the participant are key ingredients in successful relationships. It may be that the PA is perceived as the one safe human to whom the participant can truly state his or her feelings. Or it may be a combination of both. From future studies, CCL expects to understand better the ramifications of the trust perceived and embedded in this relationship.

How to Be an Effective Process Advisor

Through application or invitation, the PAs selected for LeaderLab enter a screening process that includes an in-depth look at the knowledge they bring; their style of interaction as it relates to the assessment, challenge, and support model described previously; and their understanding and commitment to the six- to nine-month process. After a number of years of working with PAs in LeaderLab, CCL began to ask what they brought to the table as individuals that made them effective. As the following thoughts from a PA demonstrate, it is necessary that the individual who undertakes this role be an experienced professional in the human development and adult learning field:

> For a process advisor to be effective he must be grounded in the program goal, content, and assessment materials used; be competent in understanding adult learning and development, especially as it relates to the work context; have the ability to understand business context through real experience and/or broad exposure; be able to create rapport and sustain trusting relationships; and have the ability to understand meeting goals as a dynamic process. For me, the image is a professional person who can meet a client on a competent level of language and dialogue. Humor and flexibility [are needed] as well as the ability to hold someone accountable to a mutually respectful relationship.

LeaderLab staff who have worked with PAs over several years also have insightful observations about what makes for an effective PA, as well as recommendations for developing the effectiveness of PAs.

The Three Keys of Effective Process Advisors

Effective PAs share three attributes: knowledge, a supportive style, and availability.

Knowledge. Effective process advisors have a thorough understanding of human development and adult learning processes. They have the appropriate educational background and the ability to use counseling skills to encourage dialogue and allow the individual participant to surface and work through challenges and issues. Their educational background and experience enables them to understand management and organizational and systems development issues. They must be credible to the advisee and bring to the relationship some experience with working in or with organizations.

The effective PA is also well trained in the goals and intent of advising work, implicitly understands the tools used in the process, and is facile in making connections and aiding the advisee in taking action or making the personal changes that may be difficult because those actions involve changing ingrained behavioral patterns linked to long-held beliefs or traits that are reinforced at work or home.

Supportive Style. The successful PA works within the guidelines of the program, yet deals with the evolution of the process as new information is introduced. Although their personal styles vary as they meet this goal, effective PAs share some central abilities and values, including a motivation to teach others, keen observation skills, a knowledge of how to encourage action and when to pause, an ability to sense the personal issues underlying the development situation, and a strong desire to help others grow and change.

No one particular PA personality or style is best. Some people are more naturally talented than others in serving the roles associated with a coaching relationship; however, many of the effectiveness skills can be developed, especially if they are coupled to clearly defined goals, parameters, and expectations. The individual personalities of process advisors vary widely, yet, in a long-term study of LeaderLab, the PA role consistently received a value rating of 4.8 measured on a 5-point scale (Young & Dixon, 1996).

Availability. All coaching processes take time. Effective process advisors commit twenty-five to thirty hours to each individual advisee. This time commitment is regarded as an integral part of the developmental work, and must be adhered to even when the advisee is juggling a heavy travel and work schedule, and even if calls and contacts must be frequently shifted.

To make this time commitment possible, the process advisor focuses on two to three advisees in each LeaderLab program for the six- to nine-month period. To maintain effectiveness, a process advisor's program assignments are limited to a specific number of advisees during any given period. The PA is analogous to the flight controller at a busy airport, who can have only so many planes in the air at once to perform effectively. For example, if a PA is working with three individuals in three programs, that PA is working with nine advisees at three different stages of developmental learning.

An effective PA manages the time constraints and the time commitments by adhering to a carefully constructed plan of action and contact that includes preparing for the first face-to-face encounter by reviewing all the prework assessments; making phone calls as agreed upon by advisee and the PA; making the many "phone-tag" calls that occur as advisee schedules change; preparing for each call by reviewing notes, action plans, and the current journal submissions; preparing for the second face-to-face meeting; conducting two face-to-face meetings (set three months apart—the second coming when participants return for the second phase of the classroom work); having several conversations with the LeaderLab program manager around the status of the PA's relationship with the advisee; and determining any program support actions that might be needed.

Developing Effective Process Advisors

CCL believes the PA process is a two-way street. It cannot have effective and successful PAs if it does not also educate, support, and coach them. CCL does these things in a number of ways: training, frequent communication, quarterly meetings and an annual retreat, and peer reviews.

Training. A two- to three-day training program is held for PAs to teach the program goal, the competencies, the expectations, and the instruments of their craft. In addition, PAs go through a practice session that is observed for the purpose of selection and further coaching. The PAs are provided with a very clear and structured set of instructions, affectionately known as the *PA Waltz,* that covers in detail what needs to be done over the several months that comprise the development process. The instructions include such information as guidelines for preparing for each phone call and for the one-on-one meetings. PAs also receive a form to use with their advisees for scheduling the telephone contacts, suggested journal input questions, and a journal review sheet to help in preparing for each call.

Frequent Communications. The PA and program staff have frequent contact that includes advice on how to get the advisee to respond to calls or to e-mails, provides a means of exchanging ideas and questions, and allows for a sharing of tactics that have worked for other PAs.

Quarterly Meetings and Yearly Retreat. Each of these meetings has a specific focus and is meant to help PAs and program managers learn from each other and contribute to a general knowledge about the process. The yearly retreat keeps the staff updated on the latest program innovations and thinking and provides additional learning and community-building opportunities. Sharing stories, experiences, problems, and concerns increases each PA's understanding of the program methodology and enhances his or her effectiveness.

Peer Reviews. Reviewing each other's work and techniques is used as a learning and coaching tool for PAs. The PAs discuss their work with one another in review teams, thus expanding the knowledge base of each member of the team as well as providing assessment, challenge, and support to each other. These peer-review processes have been especially valuable over time. As a PA works with a number of individuals from the same organization, he or she becomes knowledgeable about a particular industry and its unique needs. This PA then becomes a valuable resource and coach for other PAs when they work with advisees from that industry.

What We Have Learned About Process Advising

The day-to-day program activity in LeaderLab along with the forums, quarterly meetings, and yearly retreats have generated a number of learnings and best practices about process advising. Work is currently underway that will formally document this information. For now, however, I offer a compilation of stories and informal shared knowledge from individual PAs. Here are some of the themes that have arisen through observation and the gathering of anecdotal evidence.

Process Advising Is Different from Executive Coaching

Process advising blends face-to-face dialogue with telephone work. It is different from executive coaching, which occurs mostly in one-on-one interactions conducted usually at very senior levels for a select few and which seems to carry a greater sense of urgency for the organization's strategic success. Process advising, because of its focus and design, is available to a larger number of people. In one sense it is for the "masses," that is, for people in upper management or on high-potential tracks.

Process advising seems less intense than executive coaching. This may be because it operates within a specified time and a structural framework that includes a clearly articulated intent with specified goals for the developmental relationship, a set of competencies to use as reference points, and a focus on what the advisee's situation demands. This creates an interaction in which the advisee selects the situations or issues to be worked on and, with the guidance of the PA, develops an ongoing action plan.

Because of the limited face-to-face time, the PA does not usually have the added benefit of being able to "read" the nonverbal signals that can inform questions or dialogue. The PA does receive the advisee's journal entries prior to each phone conversation and can use that material to understand what's been occurring in the three to four weeks between calls. Participants often remark that the second face-to-face meeting is extremely useful because it is an opportunity to reconnect and focus on what has gone on in the last three months. Advisees also say that the verbal one-on-one feedback lets them connect with their PA in ways that phone calls and e-mail do not. Young's research (1996) bears out these remarks and indicates that three months is the about longest that the relationship can be enthusiastically kept alive over the telephone.

That learning was recently reconfirmed when an organization going through a merger asked CCL to design a program in which long-distance PA work lasted for six months, followed by a second face-to-face session with the participants at their jobs designed to prepare for another six months of long-distance process advising. After about three and one-half months, interactions began to deteriorate. Conference-call appointments with PAs fell off and journal submissions decreased. Advisees who did make their calls expressed a sense of dejection and frustration and questioned what was happening in the organization and what impact they could possibly have.

At the request of the client, the second face-to-face meeting was moved up in the schedule. The participants were then able to refocus and reenergize. They continued their learning process by conducting their own daylong meeting to establish operating norms and guidelines for the group.

Process Advising Requires Advisee Readiness

The typical advisee comes from upper management ranks with twelve or so years of successful experience in the organization. Potential advisees must be serious about looking at themselves and their leadership situations with the intent to make changes and take action. They must be willing to work for the entire length of the PA commitment to reap the benefits of the PA relationship.

Readiness factors and the ability to learn from experience differentiate those advisees who are able to maximize the use of their PA advocacy from those who find it merely acceptable or think of it as another organization-sponsored experience. Readiness factors refer to preexisting conditions that significantly affect whether the advisee is prepared for, or open to, the commitment and hard work required to gain the most from the PA relationship. Two significant readiness factors are external and internal stressors.

External stressors include job demands like promotions, mergers, and business pressures; pressures from bosses and co-workers to change ineffective behaviors; and big leaps in job scope. For example, as the result of a merger shortly before he entered the program and PA relationship, one advisee had moved from managing 15 people to managing over 150 and had also assumed large budget responsibilities. This increased scope and scale of the job created developmental pressure (Ruderman, Ohlott, & McCauley, 1990).

A participant's internal stressors tend to come from a dissatisfaction with work or, more generally, with life. For example, one advisee stated that he had accomplished what he wanted to do in his business. His expressed dissatisfaction was with his current perceived lack of job demands (Young & Dixon, 1993).

Learning from experience means recognizing when new behaviors, skills, or attitudes are called for. It requires the participant to engage in a variety of developmental experiences to learn new skills, try new approaches, test previously untested skills, and develop and use a variety of learning tactics (Van Velsor & Guthrie, 1998).

The Process Advisor Provides a Safe Environment

Confidentiality, trust, and a sense of safety and security are essential to the advisee's taking more effective actions. Because the PA comes from outside the organization, participants can feel free in discussing issues, with no threat of repercussions. Especially as the participant will be performing self-assessment and reviewing various assessments and 360-degree instruments completed by boss, peers, and subordinates, the PA's outsider status becomes a necessary support mechanism.

The Process Advisor Must Understand the Advisee's Situation

To a great extent, the success of the PA-advisee relationship depends on the ability of the PA to listen well—to fully understand rather than just demonstrate expertise and experience. The PA must be careful not to set up a competition with the advisee or to create an expectation that he or she has all the answers. Rather, the PA must create an environment that builds trust, which means remaining nonjudgmental and establishing a comfortable rapport so that confidences are easily shared.

Process Advising Is Real-time Support

At its best, process advising includes a practical understanding of the work environment and situation. This allows the PA to help the advisee wrestle with the dynamic tension between what the situation calls for and what the advisee is striving to do as an individual, group/team leader, or member of an organization. It allows the PA to help participants decide what questions they need to be asking when they are surrounded by change and disequilibrium, when they themselves may be feeling anxious about the future.

The Process Advisor Provides On-time Action Learning

The PA is able to use each exchange, whether it is a conversation, the scheduling of calls, or a voice or e-mail, as a potential learning aid as the individual works on his or her action plan. The PA promotes action learning in the present, working on living problems or situations and using conversations and interactions as they occur.

The Process Advisor Blends Candor and Belief in the Advisee

It is widely said that the best communication is both totally honest and totally kind at once. The PA blends both of these traits in every conversation. The most effective PA is like a mirror, reflecting both the positive and the negative aspects of the participant's situation and development. Less-successful PAs tend to be those who flinch or hedge their bets. The helpful PA is clear, direct, and honest, and recognizes that the advisee is dealing with tough issues. The general consensus among PAs is that every individual advisee needs to feel that the PA is one hundred percent in his or her corner and stands there to support his or her success.

CCL sees differences between the PA's work with individuals in an open-enrollment program (where individuals come from many organizations) and the PA's work with advisees attending a client-specific program (where the participants are all from the same organization). For example, in an open-enrollment program, the jump-off point in the first face-to-face meeting may be more relaxed and exploratory. In one participant's words: "Many of the feelings and insights I had during the week came together at the PA session. She was a good listener and helped me to unload some of my emotional load and to understand what I needed to do in the future to change and achieve some of the action plans that I need to accomplish."

In client-specific programs, the first meeting and discussion between advisee and PA is more formal and task driven. It can sometimes take the first three months for the advisee to become comfortable with the PA. Often in these situations, the second face-to-face meeting is the most useful because it provides an opportunity to focus on what has gone on in the previous three months from different perspectives. At this point, the PA is able to help the advisee on specific actions he or she could take in the coming months. The PA can also help the advisee to assimilate the new ideas that come from new information in the workplace, the program, and the PA-advisee dialogue.

The Process Advisor Works with the Changes the Advisee Wants to Make

This seems like an obvious learning. However, because we bring preconceptions to whatever we do, frequently it is easier for PAs to see from outside the situation what the participant needs to do than it is for them to listen to the participant's view of his or her own development. The PA best succeeds, however, by refraining from telling, instead questioning the advisee to invoke the ideas, dreams, and beliefs that make up the advisee's internal motivation and permit the advisee to carry out his or her action plans (Van Velsor & Guthrie, 1998).

From the external motivation perspective, knowledge that the PA is following up on progress is a stimulant for individuals to keep their development work if not on a steady boil at least on a high simmer. Occasionally someone is not motivated to stay in contact or engage. The PA may pursue several alternatives in this event, but in the end must respect the level of participation desired by the advisee and must remain professional about keeping the PA commitment to the participant.

Process Advising Makes the Most of the Advisor-Advisee Pairing

The PA methodology has three modes: reality (assessment and feedback); hope (possibilities); and learning process (structure, steps, stress management, and safety). PAs report that the holistic nature of their work arises in part from the ongoing relationships between themselves and their advisees and from the counselor aspects of that relationship.

That is not to say, however, that there are no instances in which the first contact between the PA and advisee does not go well. In some cases the advisee reports not wanting to work with the assigned PA at all, stating that the relationship feels more adversarial than supportive. In each of those cases, CCL encourages the participant to try for at least three months to work with the assigned PA, even if the advisee feels it's a bad match because of personal differences (a subtle focus on the competency of interpersonal relations and the challenge of diversity). In all such cases, reports after the first month or so indicated the work was going well; by three months, the relationship was thriving and beneficial. A few of these difficult-at-first cases have even resulted in the advisee's retaining the PA concept as part of a continuing development plan after the formal end of the program.

The Process Advisor Establishes Clear Expectations and a Framework

The program's goal and competencies, as well as the two driving questions used in this process, have proved to be an invaluable aid for helping participants remain focused on what they want to achieve. One advisee framed it this way:

> I could tell from our first phone conversation that my PA would be a good person to work with and that was more than confirmed. It impressed me that he was as emphatic about what he could not do for me as he was about what he could do for me. The challenge is mine, the process is mine, the accomplishment, if there be any, is mine. In short, there is a lot of work for me to do. It's up to me. But I have good support in my PA, and through the change partner plan I have devised, I will develop good support back home. As my PA helped me see, it is up to me.

(See Appendix E for other comments from participants and Appendix F for a case study of one participant's experience with process advising.)

Provided that the PA relationship rests on the foundation of readiness, support, and clear expectations, participants can gain significant important outcomes. In reports gleaned from the experience of participants, beneficial results included:

• Self-empowerment, a more conscious application of one's own core values and driving forces in leadership roles.

- An ability to view leadership and one's roles as leader differently.
- Composure under stress.
- A greater focus on systems-level interventions, a greater understanding of forces affecting organizations around the world and their relevance to one's own work in organizations.
- An improved understanding of diverse people and viewpoints, a heightened awareness and appreciation of differing values and mental models and of the ways they add strength to teams and organizations.
- Greater flexibility, an enhanced ability to visualize individual and organizational possibilities and to engage others in developing a shared vision.
- A commitment to continuous learning.

Other Uses for Process Advising

David Noer stated in his book *Healing the Wounds: Overcoming the Trauma of Layoffs and Revitalizing Downsized Organizations* (1993) that the "ings" are changing. Meeting the challenges of rapid change and competition is moving the language of leadership from controlling, evaluating, directing, and telling to helping, empowering, coaching, and listening.

That language rings true whether one is dealing with today's managers, baby boomers, or Generation Xers, says Ron Zemke (1996). *Boss* is a four-letter word and bossing is out—coaching is in.

Clearly, it is imperative that managers have access to varied and continuous development support avenues that can help them stay abreast of the complicated issues that beset organizations today. Following are some suggestions for enlarging CCL's process advising experiences to provide a road map to those new avenues of leadership development and to the challenges that lie ahead.

To Nurture Developmental Relationships and Systems

In the past, organizations have used just-in-time coaching (when an individual is not prepared for an assignment and receives help on the spot) and communication coaching (coaching to develop interpersonal or presentation skills). However, as CCL continues to learn from the process advisor model of coaching, it is focusing on a number of different alternatives and approaches. The following suggestions take the action learning concept at the heart of the process advising methodology into different developmental environments with separate intentions, demands, and situations.

Executive Facilitator. An experienced executive from one region is trained and then assigned to provide expertise and knowledge to a newly placed executive in another region. In this instance, facilitator and participant interact with each other during the training portion of the program. The facilitator makes site visits and is available for the entire year to help the participant make progress.

Transition Guides. Experienced process facilitators provide consistent, ongoing development support to individuals and teams. In this long-term program design, the transition guides work with designated organizations, providing face-to-face dialogue through regularly scheduled meetings.

To Maximize New Technologies

Compared to face-to-face advising, various technologies (video conferencing, the Internet, e-mail, the telephone, and distance learning, to name a few) let organizations reach a greater number of managers for a relatively small financial investment and with less time away from work.

But technology itself will not fulfill developmental and learning needs. The challenge lies not just in adopting technology but in designing the use of available technology in a way that maintains the human interaction that is a fundamental part of any manager's or leader's job. What new behaviors and interacting styles are required to communicate clearly when there are limited verbal clues and minimal visual clues to help interpret meaning? CCL knows, from its experience with process advising, that three months is about the limit for maintaining an effective advising relationship over the telephone. Further study and experience is required to determine the effective time range of other kinds of communications technology.

To Support Strategic Goals

Executive education and leadership development can have a powerful positive impact on corporate performance. For that to happen, the organization must have a well-defined, well-aligned set of strategic imperatives. This strategic agenda then serves as the basis for the establishment of various development processes that facilitate progress toward the future (Vicere & Fulmer, 1997).

In what ways does the process advising or coaching methodology support an organization's strategy? In what ways does it reinforce their development systems? One challenge is to craft action learning support roles in the context of a goal, allowing for honest grappling with a defined direction or specific issues.

Another challenge remains in finding ways to maximize the use of a process advising methodology while at the same time requiring the advisee to rapidly respond to an ever-changing environment. As one participant stated: "The PA sessions were most helpful. What kept getting in the way was the quantity and quality of change I underwent at home as well as at work and the number of brush fires that my boss required I personally put out."

To Set Action Plans or Development Plans

Process advising has been used as a support tool for setting development plans, which are then reviewed with the manager and refined as necessary. To gain a better understanding of what people require from organizations to remain effective, several questions need answering: To what extent do organizational goals extend into the arena of leadership development? How can organizations use the support supplied by process advisors to match goals and strategy expectations? How can process advising be used to monitor performance? Should process advising be used to monitor performance?

Is Process Advising Right for Your Organization?

Trust and confidentiality are important to a developmental relationship. How can an organization develop a system that both develops and provides the necessary feedback and information for future planning and succession? Is process advising the right tool for the job? Companies should examine their needs closely, and determine if long-term coaching possibilities exist within the present organizational structure.

Companies must also consider, whether these developmental roles are performed internally or externally, the time and financial commitments this type of development requires of an organization. These costs include the time necessary to evaluate and thoughtfully plan what is expected from the advising sessions and developing methods in order to ensure quality in every relationship. If, for example, the executives in an organization are asked to coach or mentor, they need more than a short briefing and a report on the value of this type of development. Those asked to play these roles will need to be educated on how to be effective in this type of role, and they must be willing and able to give sufficient time to the assignment if the development task is to be successful for both parties in the relationship and, ultimately, the organization. Figure 2 provides a sequential model, based on the Center's experience with developing the process advisor role.

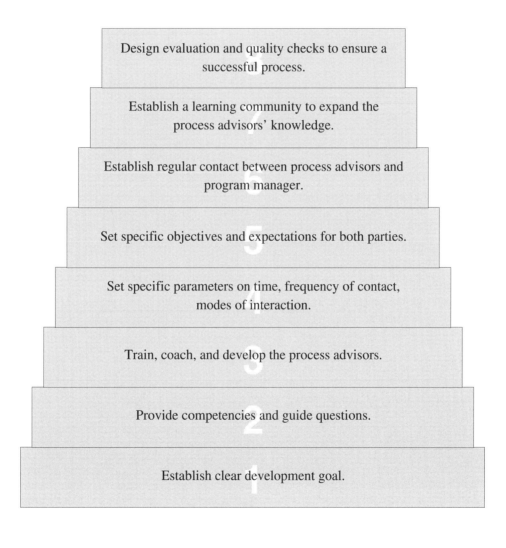

Figure 2
CCL Development of the PA Process

A Brief Exercise for Determining the Suitability of Process Advising

Using Table 4 as a guide to the process advisor roles, an organization can pose the following developmental relationship questions to make a quick analysis of how it might use process advising to advance developmental relationships.

First, the organization should ask what it is that needs enhancing: Is it learning and development for organization members, business or strategic development, technological development, or some combination of these? Who and what types of coaching situations would be most effective for the various needs? What types of advisor education would each require?

An organization should also consider these questions in its examination of a possible developmental relationship system:

- What are the similarities and differences between roles?
- Which roles naturally occur in the organization?
- How frequently and to what extent do they occur?
- Who plays these roles—the immediate boss? An expert? Informal or formal mentors? Peers?
- Where are the gaps in the developmental roles in the organization?
- Of these gaps, which can be filled through human resources functions, be filled through outside experts, or be taught to managers?
- Which roles require confidentiality or the security provided by outside process advisors?

Alternative and Adjunct Roles for Internal Long-term Advising

In addition, or as an alternative, to the PA, others in the organization can play roles and take responsibilities to create a successful development process:

Sponsor/Manager. Responsibilities for this role include setting the strategy for the process, determining with the advisee what is needed from the developmental experience, showing constancy of interest; meeting the advisee before the advising process begins and then monthly after each of the advising contacts at the end of the coaching period, and providing input as requested.

Human Resources. Responsibilities for this role include establishing support for changes in leadership behaviors; assessing readiness when selecting individuals for development; providing guidance to the sponsor and the advisee on what is required in each role; creating support mechanisms for the manager and advisor to ensure honest feedback, emotional support, experience, and expertise from the process and/or managerial side; and

Table 4
Roles Played by Process Advisors in Developmental Relationships

Element	*Role*	*Function*
ASSESSMENT	Feedback provider	Raises awareness of skill deficiencies and of strengths the person is not fully utilizing.
	Reflective thinking partner	Probes assumptions; provides different perspectives for clarifying issues.
	Expert	Offers advice, suggests strategies based on assessments and knowledge of change and development processes.
CHALLENGE	Dialogue partner	Insists that ownership of and deciding upon course of action rests with individual.
	Accountant	Motivates by asking for an accounting of progress.
SUPPORT	Role model	Demonstrates competency in modeling change and development processes.
	Counselor	Aids in understanding of emotional side of learning—frustrations of failure, fears of change, and so on.
	Positive reinforcer	Encourages; expresses confidence; acknowledges manager for making progress.
	Historian	Tracks progress, reminds of accomplishments.

Adapted from *The Center for Creative Leadership Handbook of Leadership Development* (Jossey-Bass, 1998).

ensuring confidentiality between advisee and PA if the organization uses any type of assessment.

Process Advisor. The person in this role is responsible for providing an accountability structure; behavioral expertise; encouragement; awareness of the advisee's strengths and weaknesses; and confidentiality, trust, and safety.

The Value of Process Advising

The question is sometimes raised as to how to evaluate the impact of this type of work, as tangible, bottom-line results are not easily seen. There are no simple answers. One organization involved in this process has designed preassessment of the participating employee's development path. It then uses the coaching process and sets performance goals that can be measured at performance review time. This organization is still evaluating the success of this approach.

A number of other organizations are working to develop systems that can verify what remains a rather intangible benefit for an organization—human development. CCL is currently working on an evaluation toolkit to help answer some of these questions, and it continues to do research on the learnings, best practices, and development of process advising and of various other types of coaching models.

References

Burnside, R. M., & Guthrie, V. A. (1992). *Training for action: A new approach to executive development.* Greensboro, NC: Center for Creative Leadership.

Cell, E. (1984). *Learning to learn from experience.* Albany: State University of New York.

Gryskiewicz, S. S. (1999). *Positive turbulence: Developing climates for creativity, innovation, and renewal.* San Francisco: Jossey-Bass.

McCauley, C. D., & Hughes-James, M. W. (1994). *An evaluation of the outcomes of a leadership development program.* Greensboro, NC: Center for Creative Leadership.

McCauley, C. D., Moxley, R. S., & Van Velsor, E. (Eds.). (1998). *The Center for Creative Leadership handbook of leadership development.* San Francisco: Jossey-Bass.

Noer, D. M. (1993). *Healing the wounds: Overcoming the trauma of layoffs and revitalizing downsized organizations.* San Francisco: Jossey-Bass.

Petranek, C. F., Corey, S., & Black, R. (1992). Three levels of learning in simulations: Participating, debriefing, and journal writing. *Simulation and Gaming, 23*(2), 174-185.

Ruderman, M. N., Ohlott, P. J., & McCauley, C. D. (1990). Assessing opportunities for leadership development. In K. E. Clark & M. B. Clark (Eds.), *Measures of leadership* (pp. 547-562). West Orange, NJ: Leadership Library of America.

Sayles, L. R. (1993). *The working leader.* New York: Free Press.

Van Velsor, E., & Guthrie, V. A. (1998). Enhancing the ability to learn from experience. In C. D. McCauley, R. S. Moxley, & E. Van Velsor (Eds.), *The Center for Creative Leadership handbook of leadership development* (pp. 242-261). San Francisco: Jossey Bass.

Vicere, A. A., & Fulmer, R. M. (1997). *Leadership by design.* Boston, MA: Harvard Business School Press.

Wills, S. (1994). 2001: A research odyssey. *Journal of Management Development, 13*(1), 60-72. (Bradford, West Yorkshire, England: MCB University Press.)

Young, D. P., & Dixon, N. M. (1993). *Using evaluation to build leadership development programs.* Paper presented at the annual meeting of the American Evaluation Association, Dallas, TX.

Young, D. P., & Dixon, N. M. (1996). *Helping leaders take effective action: A program evaluation.* Greensboro, NC: Center for Creative Leadership.

Young, D. P., & Hefferan, J. (1994). *LeaderLab program feedback report.* Unpublished manuscript, Center for Creative Leadership, Greensboro, NC.

Zemke, R. (1996, December). The corporate coach. *Training, 33*(12), 24-28.

Suggested Reading

Conger, J. (1992). *Learning to lead: The art of transforming managers into leaders.* San Francisco: Jossey-Bass.

Dalton, M. A., & Hollenbeck, G. P. (1996). *How to design an effective system for developing managers and executives.* Greensboro, NC: Center for Creative Leadership.

Denison, D. R., & Mishra, A. K. (1995, March-April). Toward a theory of organizational culture and effectiveness. *Organization Science, 6*(2), 204-223.

Douglas, C. A. (1997). *Formal mentoring programs in organizations: An annotated bibliography.* Greensboro, NC: Center for Creative Leadership.

Kaplan, R. E., & Palus, C. J. (1994). *Enhancing 360-degree feedback for senior executives.* Greensboro, NC: Center for Creative Leadership.

Leider, R. J. (1985). *The power of purpose.* New York: Ballantine.

McCauley, C. D., & Young, D. P. (1993). Creating developmental relationships: Roles and strategies. *Human Resource Management Review, 3*(3), 219-230.

Sayles, L. R. (1989). *Leadership: Managing in real organizations.* New York: McGraw-Hill.

Witherspoon, R., & White, R. P. (1997). *Four essential ways that coaching can help executives.* Greensboro, NC: Center for Creative Leadership.

Appendix A
Description of the LeaderLab Program

The LeaderLab program begins with six days at CCL. Participants receive feedback on their assessments and co-worker evaluations, meet with their PAs, learn from lectures and discussions, and engage in a number of experiential and nontraditional learning activities. They develop relationships with *change partners* within the participant group. Change partners, working in groups of three, provide support for each other and process with each other what they are learning.

Developing an action plan is key to the program, and the process takes participants through several steps, ranging from guided visualization to the development of a written plan for action. This plan typically includes several statements that prescribe taking specific actions, such as focusing on the needs of external and internal customers or focusing on achieving balance in work and personal life. As part of the plan the participant is asked to provide concrete short- and long-term goals. He or she attains success through meeting these goals.

After the initial six days, the participant returns to work for three months and implements his or her action plan. Each keeps a learning journal, which is used for reflection and for communication with the PA, and establishes a second set of change partners in the work environment, people who provide support and feedback for the actions the participant is working on. PAs contact participants by phone at least once each month to support and challenge their efforts to become more effective.

At the end of the three months, the participants return to CCL for four days to process their learning and again participate in various classroom activities. They spend time with their PAs and revise their action plans, taking into account what has been learned in the first three months. After the second session, participants work to implement their revised plans during the two-and-a-half remaining months of the program. They continue to engage in journal writing, interact with their back-home change partners, and talk with their PAs as a way to reflect on their actions and garner support.

The program ends after six months, at which time the participant provides an in-depth written summary of the experience and has a final conversation with the PA. An annual network meeting of all program alumni is held to provide continued support and learning.

Appendix B
Learning Journals: A Means for Reflecting on Practice

Learning journals, in which program participants document events and record important issues during time away from class, facilitate later contact between participant and process advisor. Reports of the benefits of learning journals include enhancing reflective thinking skills; distilling lessons from experience; encouraging self-analysis that is independent of the classroom; and tracking learning, important lessons, trends, and patterns over time (Cell, 1984; McCauley & Hughes-James, 1994; Petranek, Corey, & Black, 1992; Wills, 1994; Young & Hefferan, 1994). The journals, which are routinely sent to the PA and provide much of the subject matter for phone conversations, are personal and confidential. No one but the PA ever sees a journal unless the participant chooses to share it with another staff member.

Appendix C
Participant Essay on the Tools of the Program

My journey into the world of LeaderLab coincided with my conversion from a fairly secure employee at a local college to a risk-taking entrepreneur. During the last months of summer, a packet of LeaderLab preprogram materials arrived. I opened the envelope with a variety of emotions which ranged from elation to curiosity, anticipation to anxiety, and confidence to trepidation. After I watched the videotaped message and went over the instruments, this catalyst for a major change in my life was filed away. After all, I had nearly three weeks to complete the materials!

When I finally sat down to work on my packet, a delightful and frightening pattern emerged. The instruments referred me back to myself on all levels. The Sense of Purpose and Mission Statement were the basis of my business plan. Examining my critical incidents and their impact upon me led to a myriad of reflections upon my decision. Even the act of selecting observers for the multi-rater forms became an exercise in identifying and forming a core network for my fledgling company.

Working with the process advisor helped me confirm what the instruments were saying—that I met the parameters for an entrepreneur. My FIRO-B and other instruments gave me quantifiable data for my dream. It was through the process advising session and phone calls that I was able to redirect my "feet," clarify my plan ("head") and act from the "heart." My tradeoffs are easier to apply because I know enough about myself to handle the disequilibrium which comes with personal and professional change.

The journal has served two distinct purposes for me. Because of the reflective nature of journaling, I am less critical of myself and others. I have also learned to extract "pearls of wisdom" from the learnings. I discovered a different way to approach the problem or was able to "cut my losses" without feeling a sense of loss. My process advisor and I concur that I have grown and changed in a very positive and noticeable manner over these six months—and my change partners agree.

Prior to our work together, I believed that I was fairly visionary and creative. I also knew that because of my propensity for dreaming, the nuts-and-bolts work for implementation of details to actualize the dream was not a part of my modus operandi. My process advisor helped me to realize that my global perspective often kept me from adequate examination of the mundane building blocks and philosophies important to building and sustaining my vision. We worked on starting small and growing big. In other words, rather than focusing upon the entire jigsaw puzzle of life, I can examine and refine the individual pieces before I proceed to try to interlock them.

The insights I garnered over the first three months were obvious in others as I returned for the second session. Listening to my peers and watching their developmental level was a reaffirmation of my personal growth. I was cognizant of a gain in confidence, listening skills, and open and honest feedback.

My process advisor never allowed me to think or speak in generalities. He constantly pushed me to the edge of my comfort zone and let me know about my growth as horizons expanded. During the early months when I was refining my personal skills, he would hone in on any insecurities. I jokingly called him my "personal laser."

My development path has no finish line. I learned throughout this process. I am learning to listen to suggestions for changes in my new entrepreneurial work with increased confidence and receptiveness. I do not feel threatened by individuals who have attained successful rungs on the corporate ladder. Listening to them, interacting with them and motivating young adults during workshops has brought me to the attention of several "movers and shakers." These individuals not only become a part of the different strong network but templates for what to do and what not to do. Cultural enrichment is often an expensive process and the diverse nature of our class was a laboratory within itself.

My final and most important "aha" resulted from the journal. I learned that the process of sharing my thoughts, feelings and philosophies worked for me. The PA's reception of these musings has affirmed my ability to write for publication. I do plan to submit a compilation of these entries as a published manuscript. I will use this gift from God—the ability to paint pictures with a pen—to spread my message.

Appendix D
Examples of Process Advisor Roles in Action

Feedback Provider

Ronnie had seldom taken the time to examine his life, his impact on others, or his personal beliefs to the extent he did while working with his process advisor and the six-month program. He reported: "While my mistakes were, indeed, learning opportunities, the opportunity to receive the feedback from superiors, peers and subordinates was powerful in understanding how [my] style is actually perceived. The development path I choose this time will probably not involve going back to school or changing jobs, but rather seeking new ways to grow and learn while I maintain some stability in my life. . . . I understand that I often come across as a self-confident person, but deep inside I was always filled with self-doubt. The open and honest feedback, the formal and informal sharing, and the camaraderie, both inside and outside the classroom, was vital to my ability to let go of most of those inhibitions and feelings. My learnings have just begun. I am continuing to read and understand more and more about what leadership truly is and is not. I have learned even more about continuing to learn and grow—both as a person and as a professional."

Expert

Carl's authoritarian style of leadership was molded by two organizations and although he didn't consider himself to be a bad leader he knew that if one played that "big stick" game long enough, he lost perspective on how others see him. "That is where the process advisor and assessment system is at its best. Not just the formal feedback but watching that 'on paper' feedback come to life in group situations brings development needs into focus." When he experienced a group interaction where he learned that an insensitive comment of his had closed down a rich discussion, the formal feedback came home in a very personal way.

Reflective Thinking Partner and Feedback Provider

"Getting the job done is no longer enough," Mark said as he reflected on his learnings from the program. "Making significant changes in one's mode of operation is always hard to do. In my case, though, it was critical. What I have learned is really not about how to be a better leader in the general sense, but how and why to change my personal habits to become a more sensitive leader. Leadership has a new meaning to me now. While there may be different ideas on how to reach that point of understanding, I certainly see things through 'different lenses.' Perhaps that is part of growth and without growth there is no progress."

Positive Reinforcer

Tom characterized himself as a successful manager, attributing much of that success to "brute force." He viewed leadership as requiring the "push-oriented directive," meaning it was the leader's job to figure out what to do and ask people to do it. Although he knew his weaknesses, he viewed them as offset by his strengths and therefore not worth focusing on. He had not attended any development or training programs in more than five years and felt his sensitivity to his own needs and those of others was limited. He believed the responsibility was his to ensure the optimal results. He came into the program looking for ways to make his job and work easier and discovered the challenges more difficult than he expected. He learned that much of leadership is about meaning and developed a personal leadership plan that includes letting others lead, building consensus, connecting with others, understanding perfection is not the goal, and sharing ideals and vision.

Counselor

"I had been in leadership positions during most stages of my life—from grade school through grad school," Ray recalled. "Once I began my business career, my leadership potential was quickly recognized and within a short time I was double jumped on the management ladder. And then, six years later, a potentially derailing situation threatened the leadership role I continued to fill—and in retrospect grew to require. A different company took over control and imposed a new value system that disregarded the skills I had acquired and practiced. The skills I had succeeded with. I fell from grace and no longer felt like the exemplary leader. The program helped me figure out a way to adapt my leadership style to changing situations and to perhaps find a way to regain what I had lost, and to hopefully help me find myself once again. The variety of challenges in the program provided me many things I needed, including opportunities to reflect with others from diverse backgrounds who empathized; new ways of looking at things; new ways of working with others (as opposed to the autocratic model I grew up with).

"I approached the learning with a bit of a split personality—listening for what could make me a generically better leader someday while listening most particularly for what could help me out of my present dilemma. The development process helped me get through the anger, the disappointment, the doubts, and empowered me once again to be myself and to search for a space I could call my own."

Dialogue Partner

"My biggest learning has been around a change in my self-esteem, a problem that has plagued me for awhile," John said, looking back on his program experience. "It took me awhile to figure out it was there, and once I discovered it, I couldn't seem to do much about it. All of the feedback I'd received over time indicated I do a great job; people like to work for me. I'm effective, a team player, have continuously moved into take-charge positions and have lots of leadership characteristics. It was during a specific program session where I became aware of my block. I wrote in my journal: 'I've been walking around my self-esteem mammoth and picking at it with small weapons. They have helped but have not gotten to the root of the problem. There is a 42 regular in this body. That's what I'd been for years prior to quitting smoking and a serious accident. It makes me uncomfortable meeting new people. I either need to lose the weight or accept myself; and it will be easier to lose the weight.'

"Today I weigh 50 pounds less than when I was with the program. I have my self-esteem back with a vengeance. It may seem strange to others, somewhat less to me, that so much of the self-esteem was connected with the weight gain, and now the loss. In hindsight, being fit has always been important to me—as was looking good. And I had been feeling neither. How does this all fit with me developing my own leadership? I really was a very respectable leader in the first place. But I didn't know that I was so good. People would tell me, but I never listened. The assessments, the challenges of the exercises and the program processes as well as the support of the instructors, coaches and classmates definitely helped me to listen to the good feedback and to take it seriously. It also indicated some areas that needed building up—largely in sharing, listening and communicating. In my last performance appraisal my boss stated how exceptionally good I had done. What is meaningful to me is that now, rather than saying he's just saying that to be nice, I know he said what he said because it is true. And I did not say 'Yes, but, I could have done it better.' I said to myself, 'I did good and he recognized it.' And next year I will do even better because I know better what needs to be done and have some tools and the confidence to help me make it happen."

Appendix E
Statements by LeaderLab Participants About Their
Process Advising Experience

"The practical help that the process advisor was able to provide was extremely helpful and useful. It was beneficial to analyze the feedback and get the perspective of someone who had no agendas."

"Without question, the most important ingredient was the PA. The discipline of sending her materials and talking to her kept me on track."

"The PA was very helpful. I felt very much encouraged. The main constraint was time. I did spend a lot of time traveling."

"The PA discussions have been by far the most useful in the process. She has followed my journey and my journal has been able to give informed feedback and suggestions on how to deal with blocks."

"My PA and I have developed a close working relationship and his feedback to me is interesting, pertinent, reinforcing and very insightful."

"Face-to-face meetings with my PA provided an opportunity for review and to begin thinking about where I'm going in the future. It was a positive, reinforcing experience rich in feedback and discussion."

"It was good to meet again face-to-face and have an opportunity to go over what has happened in the last four months between visits."

"Many of the feelings and insights that I had had during the week came together with my face-to-face session with my PA. She was a good listener and helped me to unload some of my emotional load and to understand what I needed to do in the future to change and achieve some of the action plans that I need to accomplish."

"The second face-to-face meeting was extremely useful because it provided an opportunity to focus on what has gone on the last three months, [to focus on] what specifically I can do going ahead, and to assimilate the new ideas that come from new information. Dialogue with the PA face-to-face was most important because it provided opportunity for visual as well as verbal one-on-one feedback."

"The face-to-face allows us to really connect. Doing this on the phone works only so far."

"A negative: I found myself wanting to argue with the advisor. I felt as if he was digging to make a point."

"The PA relationship was very encouraging and tended to give me a perspective that I felt had no hidden agendas."

"The PA process continues to provide me a lot of support and focus:
- Helps put things into a very logical thought process.
- Provides someone to talk out loud with; someone who helps you think and see things more clearly.
- Helped me to focus on issues that I have pushed under the carpet for a long time.
- Provides a 'safe' person to bounce ideas off.
- Provided me with clear insight and practical advice on implementing significant changes in my life.
- Lends a new pair of eyes to the data in totality.
- Provides a concentrated and focused time to work on how I can become more effective.
- [Is] helpful in terms of pulling things together and getting some important issues out on the table. My PA was a very delightful person who made me very comfortable in discussing issues that are very difficult for me. He has assisted in bringing out items that I need/want to focus on. It was a very good experience.
- [Listens to me.] It is obvious my PA has done a tremendous amount of work to prepare and condense the information down to a few key communications. He is a terrific, insightful listener.
- [Is] helpful in formulating some specific actions."

"It was obvious my PA worked very hard to get ready for me: going through mountains of notes in preparation as well as the feedback materials. She gave me a breathing image of the data from a static interpretation of the data. She had done her homework and asked excellent questions."

Appendix F
Case Study

The Context

Jim had just relocated to headquarters and at the same time was com-pleting ten years with the organization. He had spent the last seven of those ten years in a supervisory role, managing people older than he by eight to thirty years. He felt well prepared for his new assignment as he was "steeped in the authoritarian style of the organization." The entire group he worked with had spent their careers in this environment, so Jim felt it would be easy to pick up the ball and run with it. After all, everyone in the organization verified approval prior to action. There was no initiative.

However, things changed as Jim moved into his new job. He quickly got the message: "We do things differently here now." Jim spent the next three years working an average of seventy to ninety hours per week, giving up nine of the twelve weeks of vacation he had earned. The workforce was very young, which, to Jim, meant really inexperienced but willing to try anything and work hard.

A big portion of the work involved shifting the organization from its old traditions (no initiative) to a more driving focus. Jim was dealing with all kinds of situations in this work group. He knew he needed someone or something to help him, yet he still felt he was on a good personal develop-ment track.

Jim tended to move to a new job just about every three years. The time came for him to transition to another position just at the time he committed to LeaderLab and a process advisor. Something else was occurring in his life as well. At age forty he was entering a midlife transition period. As Jim weighed his decisions about where to go and what to do, he began to ask questions he'd never asked before. He found it a time of great confusion. After some long talks with his boss, with CCL researcher Dianne Young, and with the program designer, Jim decided it was okay to start the LeaderLab process despite the transition period and change in work group location and culture.

The Outcome

Jim reported learning a great deal during the six-month process, both about himself as a person and about his leadership skills. For example:

- The work transition would have been a tough process to go through by himself; adding the midlife transition to that made it doubly difficult. Having a process advisor available helped him see he was

good at what he did, and recognize that he might not always get it
perfect, but he had the tools of experience, knowledge, and good
intuition and needed to trust himself.

- Everyone is in the same boat; but most are not willing to admit how
confused or frustrated they really are.
- It was time to let go of his childhood dreams and accept where he
was and where he could go from there.
- A mentor significantly enhances chances of success in large
organizations.
- The only way to really learn is by doing it, living it.
- There are no simple formulas; it's all gray, moving fast, and you
either learn from your experiences and use the opportunities presented you (like the personal coach) or you risk failure.

Jim felt his actions had become more effective based on comments
from colleagues, subordinates, and his process advisor. His biggest surprise
working through the six-month process was that he had so much to learn
about himself if he was to be effective. His biggest disappointment was
ending the formal relationship with his PA. He reported he was very "aggres-
sive" in their first phone conversations before he accepted she was going to
be strong enough to coach him.

Future Development and Plans

Jim's current goals are to continue the process of understanding himself
and the definition of his "red dot"—his sense of purpose. He strongly feels
growth occurs from continual learning, discovery, and application.

After much reflection and dialogue with his PA, Jim recognizes and
accepts the fact that he was out in front of his organization in much of his
thinking. He recognizes his frustration but also realizes now that progress is
slow and he can be an agent for positive change, which makes him feel like
he has something to offer the organization.

He is aware of how easily he could backslide and now understands,
which he credits to the process advising process, that he tends to become
reactionary and then does less thinking about what he is saying and how it
impacts people. With his PA he created a recognition mechanism to alert him
to those situations.

As for his midlife transition, he is feeling he can control and shape the
outcome because he is knowledgeable about his purpose and where he wants
to go.

Appendix G
A Survey of Clients' Needs Around Programs

Here is what survey respondents told CCL about what they wanted from training and development and how CCL related the information to creating the process advisor role.

Provide support mechanisms that allow behavioral or situational change to take root. Frequently, when a participant returns to the workplace, he or she is immediately faced with an accumulation of work. Those with the best intention to do something differently can slip back into what is old and comfortable, even if less effective, behavior. As Aristotle said: "We are what we repeatedly do. Excellence then is not an act, but a habit."

As stated earlier, along with assessment and challenge, behavioral change requires support over time. The challenge became to create a process and provide mechanisms to make that support happen. One method was through human interaction and dialogue—the process advisor. Other support mechanisms would include the use of learning journals and change, or learning, partners. The mix within the three-person change partner groups would provide advocacy along the three lines mentioned earlier that are important for learning and change:

- Honest feedback and assessment.
- Challenge and wisdom that comes from experience.
- Support and encouragement.

Understand what the participant's situation calls for. Clients told CCL that it was important to create a program and process that would teach to context—that is, make content relevant to the individuals' situations—and to design educational programs to be more integrated, more holistic—that is, teaching not only to the cognitive side of the person but also to the emotion, values, and affect of the person and to the actions required for him or her to be effective in leadership situations.

In the holistic language of the LeaderLab program design, this meant teach not only to head (I think) but to heart and values (I feel and will) and to feet (I do). The process allows participants to articulate the situation (cognitive), clarify goals or purpose (emotional), and take action (behavioral).

Move beyond cognitive models to process and action. Clients responded that programs would be more effective if they taught to more than intellectual understanding. Thus, CCL created a learning process that moved beyond lectures, models, two-by-two matrixes, and six-step solutions, which, though useful, do not allow for the complexity and flexibility necessary today. The process would acknowledge and work through the tension between situation demands and purpose—on the individual, team/group, and organizational levels.

Leadership in Action

A publication of the
Center for Creative Leadership and
Jossey-Bass Publishers

Martin Wilcox, Editor

Leadership in Action is a bimonthly newsletter that aims to help practicing leaders and those who train and develop practicing leaders by providing them with insights gained in the course of CCL's educational and research activities. It also aims to provide a forum for the exchange of information and ideas between practitioners and CCL staff and associates.

The annual subscription price for *Leadership in Action* is $99.00 for individuals and $124.00 for institutions. To order, please contact Customer Service, Jossey-Bass Inc., Publishers, 350 Sansome Street, San Francisco, CA 94104-1342. Telephone: 888/378-2537 or 415/433-1767; fax: 800/605-2665. See the Jossey-Bass Web site at www.josseybass.com

CENTER FOR CREATIVE LEADERSHIP
New Releases, Best-sellers, Bibliographies, and Special Packages

NEW RELEASES

IDEAS INTO ACTION GUIDEBOOKS
Becoming a More Versatile Learner M. Dalton (1998, Stock #402) .... $6.95 *
Ongoing Feedback: How to Get It, How to Use It K. Kirkland & S. Manoogian (1998, Stock #400) .... $6.95 *
Reaching Your Development Goals C. McCauley & J. Martineau (1998, Stock #401) .... $6.95 *

The Center for Creative Leadership Handbook of Leadership Development C.D. McCauley,
R.S. Moxley, & E. Van Velsor (Eds.) (1998, Stock #201) .... $65.00 *
Coaching for Action: A Report on Long-term Advising in a Program Context V.A. Guthrie
(1999, Stock #181) $20.00
The Complete Inklings: Columns on Leadership and Creativity D.P. Campbell (1999, Stock #343) $30.00
**A Cross-National Comparison of Effective Leadership and Teamwork: Toward a Global
Workforce** J.B. Leslie & E. Van Velsor (1998, Stock #177) $15.00
Executive Selection: A Research Report on What Works and What Doesn't V.I. Sessa,
R. Kaiser, J.K. Taylor, & R.J. Campbell (1998, Stock #179) .... $30.00 *
Feedback to Managers (3rd Edition) J.B. Leslie & J.W. Fleenor (1998, Stock #178) .... $60.00 *
High-Performance Work Organizations: Definitions, Practices, and an Annotated Bibliography
B.L. Kirkman, K.B. Lowe, & D.P. Young (1999, Stock #342) $20.00
Internalizing Strengths: An Overlooked Way of Overcoming Weaknesses in Managers
R.E. Kaplan (1999, Stock #182) $15.00
International Success: Selecting, Developing, and Supporting Expatriate Managers M. Wilson
& M. Dalton (1998, Stock #180) .... $15.00 *
Leadership Education: A Source Book of Courses and Programs M.K. Schwartz, F.H. Freeman,
& K. Axtman (Eds.) (1998, Stock #339) .... $40.00 *
Leadership Resources: A Guide to Training and Development Tools M.K. Schwartz,
F.H. Freeman, & K. Axtman (Eds.) (1998, Stock #340) .... $40.00 *
Positive Turbulence: Developing Climates for Creativity, Innovation, and Renewal
S.S. Gryskiewicz (1999, Stock #2031) $32.95
Workforce Reductions: An Annotated Bibliography T.A. Hickok (1999, Stock #344) $20.00

BEST-SELLERS
The Adventures of Team Fantastic: A Practical Guide for Team Leaders and Members
G.L. Hallam (1996, Stock #172) $20.00
Breaking Free: A Prescription for Personal and Organizational Change D.M. Noer (1997,
Stock #271) $25.00
**Breaking the Glass Ceiling: Can Women Reach the Top of America's Largest Corporations?
(Updated Edition)** A.M. Morrison, R.P. White, & E. Van Velsor (1992, Stock #236A) $13.00
CEO Selection: A Street-smart Review G.P. Hollenbeck (1994, Stock #164) .... $25.00 *
**Choosing 360: A Guide to Evaluating Multi-rater Feedback Instruments for Management
Development** E. Van Velsor, J.B. Leslie, & J.W. Fleenor (1997, Stock #334) .... $15.00 *
Eighty-eight Assignments for Development in Place M.M. Lombardo & R.W. Eichinger
(1989, Stock #136) .... $15.00 *
**Enhancing 360-degree Feedback for Senior Executives: How to Maximize the Benefits and
Minimize the Risks** R.E. Kaplan & C.J. Palus (1994, Stock #160) .... $15.00 *
Evolving Leaders: A Model for Promoting Leadership Development in Programs C.J. Palus &
W.H. Drath (1995, Stock #165) .... $15.00 *
Executive Selection: A Look at What We Know and What We Need to Know D.L. DeVries
(1993, Stock #321) .... $20.00 *
Four Essential Ways that Coaching Can Help Executives R. Witherspoon & R.P. White (1997,
Stock #175) $10.00
A Glass Ceiling Survey: Benchmarking Barriers and Practices A.M. Morrison, C.T. Schreiber,
& K.F. Price (1995, Stock #161) $15.00
High Flyers: Developing the Next Generation of Leaders M.W. McCall, Jr. (1997, Stock #293) $27.95
How to Design an Effective System for Developing Managers and Executives M.A. Dalton &
G.P. Hollenbeck (1996, Stock #158) .... $15.00 *

If I'm In Charge Here, Why Is Everybody Laughing? D.P. Campbell (1984, Stock #205) .... $9.95 *

If You Don't Know Where You're Going You'll Probably End Up Somewhere Else
D.P. Campbell (1974, Stock #203) .... $9.95 *

The Lessons of Experience: How Successful Executives Develop on the Job M.W. McCall, Jr.,
M.M. Lombardo, & A.M. Morrison (1988, Stock #211) $27.50

A Look at Derailment Today: North America and Europe J.B. Leslie & E. Van Velsor (1996,
Stock #169) .... $20.00 *

Making Common Sense: Leadership as Meaning-making in a Community of Practice
W.H. Drath & C.J. Palus (1994, Stock #156) .... $15.00 *

Making Diversity Happen: Controversies and Solutions A.M. Morrison, M.N. Ruderman, &
M. Hughes-James (1993, Stock #320) $20.00

Managerial Promotion: The Dynamics for Men and Women M.N. Ruderman, P.J. Ohlott, &
K.E. Kram (1996, Stock #170) $15.00

Managing Across Cultures: A Learning Framework M.S. Wilson, M.H. Hoppe, & L.R. Sayles
(1996, Stock #173) $15.00

Maximizing the Value of 360-degree Feedback W.W. Tornow, M. London, & CCL Associates
(1998, Stock #295) .... $42.95 *

The New Leaders: Guidelines on Leadership Diversity in America A.M. Morrison (1992,
Stock #238A) $18.50

Perspectives on Dialogue: Making Talk Developmental for Individuals and Organizations
N.M. Dixon (1996, Stock #168) .... $20.00 *

Preventing Derailment: What To Do Before It's Too Late M.M. Lombardo & R.W. Eichinger
(1989, Stock #138) $25.00

The Realities of Management Promotion M.N. Ruderman & P.J. Ohlott (1994, Stock #157) .... $15.00 *

Selected Research on Work Team Diversity M.N. Ruderman, M.W. Hughes-James, &
S.E. Jackson (Eds.) (1996, Stock #326) $24.95

Should 360-degree Feedback Be Used Only for Developmental Purposes? D.W. Bracken,
M.A. Dalton, R.A. Jako, C.D. McCauley, V.A. Pollman, with Preface by G.P. Hollenbeck (1997,
Stock #335) .... $15.00 *

Take the Road to Creativity and Get Off Your Dead End D.P. Campbell (1977, Stock #204) .... $9.95 *

Twenty-two Ways to Develop Leadership in Staff Managers R.W. Eichinger & M.M. Lombardo
(1990, Stock #144) $15.00

BIBLIOGRAPHIES

Formal Mentoring Programs in Organizations: An Annotated Bibliography C.A. Douglas
(1997, Stock #332) $20.00

Management Development through Job Experiences: An Annotated Bibliography
C.D. McCauley & S. Brutus (1998, Stock #337) $20.00

Selection at the Top: An Annotated Bibliography V.I. Sessa & R.J. Campbell (1997, Stock #333) ... $20.00 *

Succession Planning: An Annotated Bibliography L.J. Eastman (1995, Stock #324) .... $20.00 *

Using 360-degree Feedback in Organizations: An Annotated Bibliography J.W. Fleenor &
J.M. Prince (1997, Stock #338) .... $15.00 *

SPECIAL PACKAGES

Executive Selection (Stock #710C; includes 157, 164, 179, 180, 321, 333) $85.00

Guidebook Package (Stock #721; includes 400, 401, 402) $14.95

HR Professional's Info Pack (Stock #717C; includes 136, 158, 169, 201, 324, 334, 340) $100.00

Leadership Education and Leadership Resources Package (Stock #722; includes 339, 340) $70.00

New Understanding of Leadership (Stock #718; includes 156, 165, 168) $40.00

Personal Growth, Taking Charge, and Enhancing Creativity (Stock #231; includes 203, 204, 205) $20.00

The 360 Collection (Stock #720C; includes 160, 178, 295, 334, 335, 338) $75.00

Discounts are available. Please write for a Resources catalog. Address your request to:
Publication, Center for Creative Leadership, P.O. Box 26300, Greensboro, NC 27438-6300,
336-286-4480, or fax to 336-282-3284. Purchase your publications from our on-line bookstore at
www.ccl.org/publications. All prices subject to change.

*Indicates publication is also part of a package.   7/99

ORDER FORM

Or e-mail your order via the Center's on-line bookstore at www.ccl.org

Name _____ Title _____

Organization _____

Mailing Address _____
(street address required for mailing)

City/State/Zip _____

Telephone _____ FAX _____
(telephone number required for UPS mailing)

Quantity	Stock No.	Title	Unit Cost	Amount

CCL's Federal ID Number
is 237-07-9591.

Subtotal

Shipping and Handling
(add 6% of subtotal with a $4.00 minimum;
add 40% on all international shipping)

**NC residents add 6% sales tax; CA residents add
7.75% sales tax; CO residents add 6.1% sales tax**

TOTAL

**METHOD OF PAYMENT
(ALL orders for less than $100 must be PREPAID.)**

❏ Check or money order enclosed (payable to Center for Creative Leadership).

❏ Purchase Order No. _____ (Must be accompanied by this form.)

❏ Charge my order, plus shipping, to my credit card:
　　　❏ American Express　❏ Discover　❏ MasterCard　❏ VISA

ACCOUNT NUMBER:_____ EXPIRATION DATE: MO.____ YR.____

NAME OF ISSUING BANK: _____

SIGNATURE _____

❏ Please put me on your mailing list.

**Publication • Center for Creative Leadership • P.O. Box 26300
Greensboro, NC 27438-6300
336-286-4480 • FAX 336-282-3284**

Client Priority Code: R

fold here

_____

_____

_____

CENTER FOR CREATIVE LEADERSHIP
PUBLICATION
P.O. Box 26300
Greensboro, NC 27438-6300